Rainforest Animals

By Caryn Jenner

DK | Penguin Random House

Senior Editor Carrie Love
US Senior Editor Shannon Beatty
Assistant Editor Gunjan Mewati
Senior Art Editor Rachael Parfitt
Project Art Editor Roohi Rais
Art Editor Bhagyashree Nayak
Assistant Art Editor Simran Lakhiani
Jacket Coordinator Issy Walsh
Jacket Designer Rashika Kachroo
DTP Designers Sachin Gupta, Syed Md Farhan
Picture Researcher Rituraj Singh
Production Editor Dragana Puvacic
Senior Production Controller Inderjit Bhullar
Managing Editors Penny Smith, Monica Saigal
Managing Art Editor Ivy Sengupta
Delhi Creative Heads Glenda Fernandes, Malavika Talukder
Publishing Manager Francesca Young
Deputy Art Director Mabel Chan
Publishing Director Sarah Larter

Reading Consultant Dr. Barbara Marinak
Subject Consultant Kim Dennis-Bryan

First American Edition, 2021
Published in the United States by DK Publishing
1450 Broadway, Suite 801, New York, NY 10018

Copyright © 2021 Dorling Kindersley Limited
DK, a Division of Penguin Random House LLC
21 22 23 24 25 10 9 8 7 6 5 4 3 2 1
001–321630–Dec/2021

A catalog record for this book is available from the Library of Congress.
ISBN: 978-0-7440-2650-4 (Paperback)
ISBN: 978-0-7440-2651-1 (Hardcover)

DK books are available at special discounts when purchased in bulk for sales promotions, premiums,
fund-raising, or educational use. For details, contact: DK Publishing Special Markets,
1450 Broadway, Suite 801, New York, NY 10018
SpecialSales@dk.com

Printed and bound in China

The publisher would like to thank the following for their kind permission to reproduce their photographs:
(Key: a-above; b-below/bottom; c-center; f-far; l-left; r-right; t-top)

1 Dreamstime.com: Ondřej Prosický (b). **2 Dreamstime.com:** Ernest Akayeu (tl); Dirk Ercken (bl). **3 123RF.com:** kajornyot (tr). **Dreamstime.com:**
Ernest Akayeu (t); Jens Stolt (clb); Dmitry Petlin (crb); Nilanjan Bhattacharya (b). **4 Dreamstime.com:** Ernest Akayeu (t); Dirk Ercken (bl). **5 Alamy Stock Photo:** Elena
Korchenko (tr); Octavio Campos Salles (bg). **Dreamstime.com:** Jpsdk / Jens Stolt (crb); Passakorn Umpornmaha (ca); Ondřej Prosický (cl). **6 Dreamstime.com:** Ernest Akayeu
Getty Images / iStock: Ildo Frazao (cl). **7 Dreamstime.com:** Ernest Akayeu (r). **8 Dreamstime.com:** Anankkml (bl); Ondřej Prosický (c). **8-9 Dreamstime.com:** Isselee (bc
beetles). **9 Dreamstime.com:** Iakov Filimonov (crb); Isselee (tl, clb); Slowmotiongli (cla); Titania1980 (c). **10 Dreamstime.com:** Vasilyrosca (clb). **10-11 Dreamstime.com:**
Alenakarabanova (bg). **Getty Images / iStock:** Toa55 (b). **11 Dreamstime.com:** Edwin Butter (tr); Sergey Uryadnikov (clb); Ecophoto (crb). **Getty Images / iStock:** E+ /
Global_Pics (tl). **12 Alamy Stock Photo:** H Lansdown (bc). **Dreamstime.com:** Ernest Akayeu (t). **13 Alamy Stock Photo:** imageBROKER / J & C Sohns (b); Nature Picture
Library / Andrew Walmsley (t). **14 Dreamstime.com:** Ernest Akayeu (t); Wrangel (c); Salparadis (br). **15 Dreamstime.com:** Kjersti Joergensen. **16-17 Dreamstime.com:**
Wrangel (b). **17 Alamy Stock Photo:** Minden Pictures / Murray Cooper (t). **18 Alamy Stock Photo:** Marcel Gross (b). **19 123RF.com:** Nilanjan Bhattacharya.
20 Dreamstime.com: Ernest Akayeu (t). **20-21 Alamy Stock Photo:** Biosphoto / Quentin Martinez (bc). **Dreamstime.com:** Chansom Pantip (b). **21 Dreamstime.com:** Di
Ercken (ca); Chansom Pantip (r). **22 Alamy Stock Photo:** Nature Picture Library / Bence Mate (b); Oyvind Martinsen-Panama Wildlife (c). **23 Alamy Stock Photo:** blickwinkel
Teigler (t). **24 Alamy Stock Photo:** SuperStock / RGB Ventures / Nick Garbutt (t/python). **Dreamstime.com:** Chansom Pantip (t). **24-25 Alamy Stock Photo:** Nature Pictu
Library / Daniel Heuclin. **26-27 Alamy Stock Photo:** Nature Picture Library / Lucas Bustamante (b). **Dreamstime.com:** Ernest Akayeu (t). **27 Alamy Stock Photo:** Pally (t)
28 Dreamstime.com: Ernest Akayeu (t); Marco Díaz (bc). **29 Alamy Stock Photo:** Blue Planet Archive AAF. **30 Dreamstime.com:** Ernest Akayeu (cl). **Getty Images / iSto**
Thipwan (b). **31 Getty Images / iStock:** Freder. **32 123RF.com:** Václav Šebek (b). **33 Alamy Stock Photo:** Ambling Images (t). **Shutterstock.com:** Michal Sloviak (b).
34-35 Dreamstime.com: Alenakarabanova (bg). **34 Dreamstime.com:** Isselee (br); André Labetaa (cl). **35 Dreamstime.com:** Digitalimagined (clb); Arindam Ghosh (tl)
Dennis Van De Water (cr); Charoenchai Tothaisong (b). **36 Alamy Stock Photo:** Morley Read. **Dreamstime.com:** Ernest Akayeu (t). **37 Dreamstime.com:** Ernest Akayeu (t)
Vasyl Helevachuk (clb). **38-39 Dreamstime.com:** Ernest Akayeu (t). **Getty Images:** Tim Flach (b). **39 Shutterstock.com:** Tom Black Dragon (t). **40 Dreamstime.com:** Ond
Prosický. **41 Dreamstime.com:** Dewins (bl); Jens Stolt (cb); Tzooka (br). **42-43 Dreamstime.com:** Alenakarabanova (bg). **42 Dreamstime.com:** Anankkml (cb); Dirk Ercke
(clb); Jens Stolt (bc). **43 123RF.com:** kajornyot (tl). **Dreamstime.com:** Nilanjan Bhattacharya (cb/tiger); Jens Stolt (cb); Isselee (fcrb/beetles); Vaclav Seb
(cl); Seadam (cla); Jesse Kraft (cra). **Getty Images:** Tim Flach (br). **44-45 Dreamstime.com:** Alenakarabanova (bg). **46-47 Dreamstime.com:** Alenakarabanova (bg).

Cover images: *Front:* Alamy Stock Photo: Francesco Puntiroli; *Back:* **Dreamstime.com:** Dmitry Petlin tr.

Endpaper images: *Front:* **Getty Images / iStock:** miroslav_1; *Back:* **Getty Images / iStock:** miroslav_1.

All other images © Dorling Kindersley
For further information see: www.dkimages.com

For the curious
www.dk.com

MIX
Paper from
responsible sources
FSC™ C018179

This book was made with Forest
Stewardship Council™ certified paper—
one small step in DK's commitment to
a sustainable future. For more information
go to www.dk.com/our-green-pledge

Contents

Chapter 1
What is a rainforest?

Welcome to the rainforest. This is a tropical rainforest. It is very hot and rainy here. The rainforest is full of leafy plants. Tall trees block the sunlight from reaching the forest floor. It is the perfect home for rainforest animals.

Red-eyed tree frog

Lots of different kinds of animals live in rainforests.

Amazon Rainforest

Tropical rainforests only cover a small amount of the Earth. But they are home to more than one million different kinds of animals. The biggest rainforest is the Amazon Rainforest.

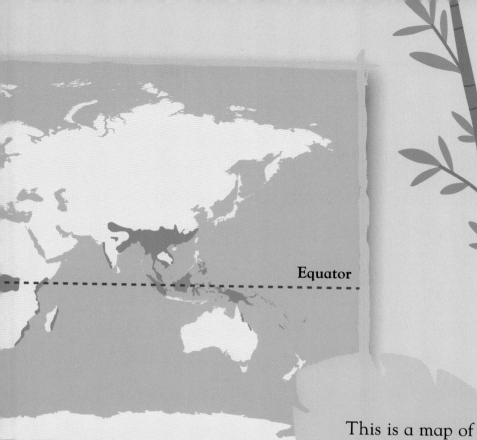

Equator

This is a map of
the world. Tropical
rainforests are
shown in green.

Tropical rainforests
are found near the
equator. The equator
is an imaginary line around
the middle of Earth.

Different kinds of animals live in different layers of the rainforest. Some animals live high up in the tops of the trees. Some animals live on the forest floor. Other animals live in the layers in between.

Understory

Sparkling violetear

Jaguar

Forest floor

Emergent layer

Green-winged macaw

Harpy eagle

Canopy

Red howler monkey

Toco toucan

Emerald tree boa

Hercules beetle

Giant anteater

9

Rainforests in danger

Humans are destroying much of the world's rainforests. Some rainforest animals are dying out. Humans must save the rainforests and the animals.

A piece of rainforest the size of a soccer field is destroyed every six seconds. The trees are often burned. The cleared land is then used to raise cattle.

Rainforest animals in danger

Jaguar
(Near threatened)

Golden lion
tamarin
(Endangered)

Orangutan
(Critically
endangered)

Bengal tiger
(Endangered)

Chapter 2
Furry animals

Sloths hang upside down from trees in the rainforest. They sleep most of the time. Zzzzzz.

Mother sloth with her baby

Slow loris

Lemurs and lorises live in the trees, too. Babies cling to their mothers until they are able to climb on their own.

Mother lemur with her baby

13

Many kinds of monkeys live in the rainforest. They climb the trees. Some monkeys are very noisy. They chatter, howl, or squeak.

Golden lion tamarin

Brown woolly monkey

Orangutan

Orangutans are apes, not monkeys. They swing between trees with their long arms. They have long orange fur. The word "orangutan" means "person of the forest."

Giant anteaters live on the forest floor. The anteater uses its long tongue to eat ants. An anteater eats about 35,000 ants and termites every day.

Tapirs also live on the forest floor. Tapirs eat plants.

Giant anteater

Lowland tapir

ROAR! Here come the big cats! Tigers, leopards, and jaguars all live in rainforests in different parts of the world. The patterns on their fur help them hide from other animals. That makes it easier for the big cats to catch their dinner.

Leopard relaxing on a tree

Bengal tiger

Tigers are the biggest and most powerful of all the big cats.

19

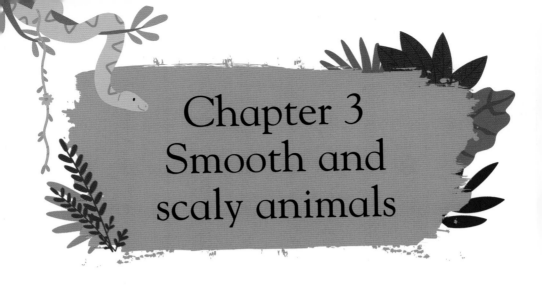

Chapter 3
Smooth and
scaly animals

Many frogs live in the rainforest.
The flying tree frog glides between
trees and down to the ground. Its
webbed toes act like a parachute.

The poison frog is very dangerous. The poison is on the frog's skin. Don't touch!

Poison frog

Flying frog

Lots of lizards live in the rainforest, too. Iguanas are large lizards with powerful tails.

Iguana

Cameroon stumptail chameleon

Chameleons change
color to blend in with
the rainforest. They hide
from other animals.
   Some rainforest lizards run
across the water. Splish, splash!

Basilisk lizard

Reticulated python

Snakes slide along the rainforest floor and slither up trees. The rainforest is home to snakes, such as anacondas and pythons. These are the longest snakes in the world.

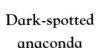

A reticulated python can regularly reach more than 20 ft (6.25 m).

Dark-spotted anaconda

Snakes have skin that is covered in scales.

25

Snap! A caiman opens its jaws wide. Caimans are a kind of alligator. They live in rivers and swamps in the rainforest.

Electric eels swim both forward and backward. They use a shock of electricity to stun and catch fish to eat.

Caiman

Electric eel

Chapter 4
Birds

Many different kinds of birds fly around the rainforest. These colorful birds are macaws. Macaws are a kind of parrot. They live together in large flocks. Macaws are very noisy. Screech! Screech!

Scarlet macaw

Scarlet macaws
can live for up to
50 years in the wild.

Toucans and hornbills both have big beaks. They use their beaks to pick fruit from the rainforest trees. They also use their beaks to catch insects and small animals.

Rhinoceros hornbill

Chestnut-mandibled
toucan

King vultures perch high up in the rainforest. They look for dead animals below. Then they fly down to eat their dinner.

King vulture

Harpy eagle

Harpy eagles eat monkeys and sloths. They have strong claws to pluck the animals from the trees.

Cassowaries cannot fly. They run along the forest floor. They eat rats and other small animals.

Southern cassowary

Unusual rainforest animals

These are some unusual animals that live in rainforests.

Hoatzins have an awful smell to keep other animals away.

Okapis have stripes like a zebra, but are related to giraffes.

Vampire bats feed on the blood of other animals.

Giraffe weevils are small beetles with a long neck.

Pangolins have scales for protection.

Chapter 5
Creepy-crawlies

Tarantula

The rainforest is alive with millions of different kinds of insects. Look out for tarantulas! These big hairy spiders eat birds, frogs, and other small animals.

Titan beetles are the biggest beetles in the world. Titan beetles have very strong jaws called mandibles.

A titan beetle is about as big as a cell phone.

Lots of ants swarm through the rainforest. Army ants are small but dangerous. They work together to attack and eat other insects and small animals.

Millions of leaf-cutter ants live together in huge nests on the forest floor. They cut leaves from plants and carry the leaves to their nest.

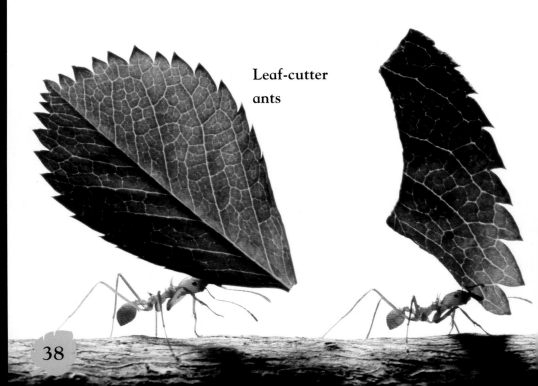

Leaf-cutter ants

Army ants

Blue morphos
are one of the
largest butterflies
in the world.

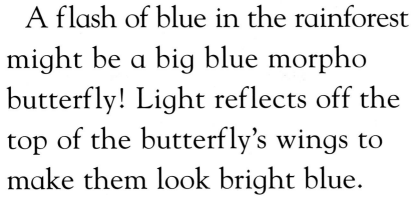

A flash of blue in the rainforest might be a big blue morpho butterfly! Light reflects off the top of the butterfly's wings to make them look bright blue. The rainforest is full of amazing animals!

A blue morpho is about as big as a human adult's hand.

Rainforest facts

Why do so many different kinds of animals make their homes in rainforests?

Rainforests have plenty of food and water for the animals.

Rainforest trees give shade from the heat. They also give shelter from the rain.

Malayan tapir

Yellow-headed poison frog

Blue morpho

Rainforest layers offer different kinds of homes for different kinds of animals.

Great hornbill

Three-toed sloth

Toco toucan

Bald uakari

Boa constrictor

Panther chameleon

Bengal tiger

New kinds of rainforest animals are still being discovered.

Hercules beetles

Leaf-cutter ants

Quiz

1 What is the biggest rainforest called?

2 What do sloths do most of the time?

3 What does the word "orangutan" mean?

4 How many ants and termites does an anteater eat every day?

5 What is on the skin of a poison frog?

6 Name two kinds of snakes that make their home in rainforests.

7   How do electric eels catch fish to eat?

8   Name two animals that harpy eagles eat.

9   What kind of bat feeds on the blood of other animals?

10   What are the largest beetles in the world?

Glossary

destroying
Ruining completely.

endangered
In danger of dying out.

equator
Imaginary line around Earth's middle.

mandibles
Jaws of a beetle.

reflects
Light that is thrown back from a surface.

slither
Move smoothly in a twisting way.

swamps
Areas of wet ground.

tropical
Hot and humid. Tropical places are close to the equator.

Index

A LEVEL FOR EVERY READER

This book is a part of an exciting four-level reading series to support children in developing the habit of reading widely for both pleasure and information. Each book is designed to develop a child's reading skills, fluency, grammar awareness, and comprehension in order to build confidence and enjoyment when reading.

Ready for a Level 2 (Beginning to Read) book

A child should:

- be able to recognize a bank of common words quickly and be able to blend sounds together to make some words.
- be familiar with using beginner letter sounds and context clues to figure out unfamiliar words.
- sometimes correct their reading if it doesn't look right or make sense.
- be aware of the need for a slight pause at commas and a longer one at periods.

A valuable and shared reading experience

For many children, reading requires much effort, but adult participation can make reading both fun and easier. Here are a few tips on how to use this book with a young reader:

Check out the contents together:
- read about the book on the back cover and talk about the contents page to help heighten interest and expectation.
- discuss new or difficult words.
- talk about labels, annotations, and pictures.

Support the reader:
- tell the child the title and help them predict what the book will be about.
- give the book to the young reader to turn the pages.
- where necessary, encourage longer words to be broken into syllables, sound out each one, and then flow the syllables together; ask the child to reread the sentence to check the meaning.
- encourage the reader to vary their voice as they read; demonstrate how to do this, if helpful.

Talk at the end of each page:
- ask questions about the text and the meaning of some of the words used—this helps develop comprehension skills.
- read the quiz at the end of the book and encourage the reader to answer the questions, if necessary, by turning back to the relevant pages to find the answers.

Reading consultant: Dr. Barbara Marinak, Dean and Professor of Education at Mount St. Mary's University, Maryland.

48